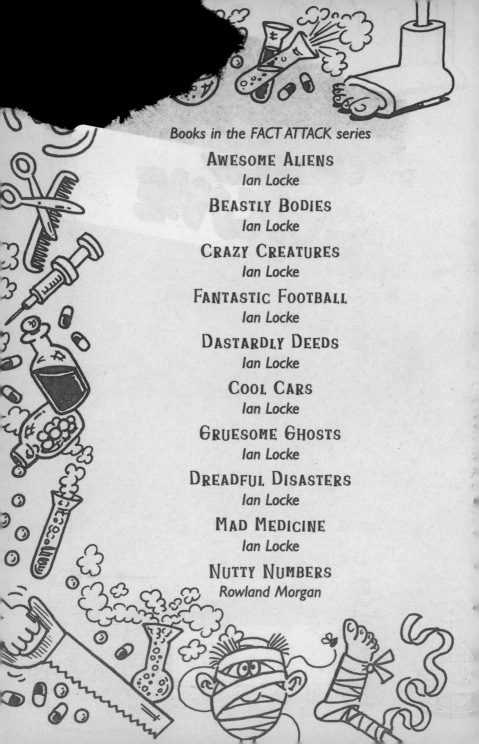

Books in the FACT ATTACK series

FACT ATTACK

MAD MEDICINE

Ian Locke

MACMILLAN CHILDREN'S BOOKS

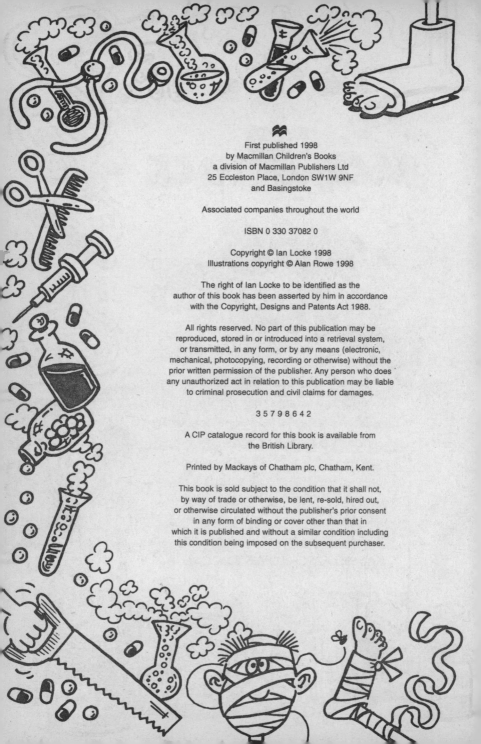

First published 1998
by Macmillan Children's Books
a division of Macmillan Publishers Ltd
25 Eccleston Place, London SW1W 9NF
and Basingstoke

Associated companies throughout the world

ISBN 0 330 37082 0

3 5 7 9 8 6 4 2

A CIP catalogue record for this book is available from
the British Library.

Printed by Mackays of Chatham plc, Chatham, Kent.

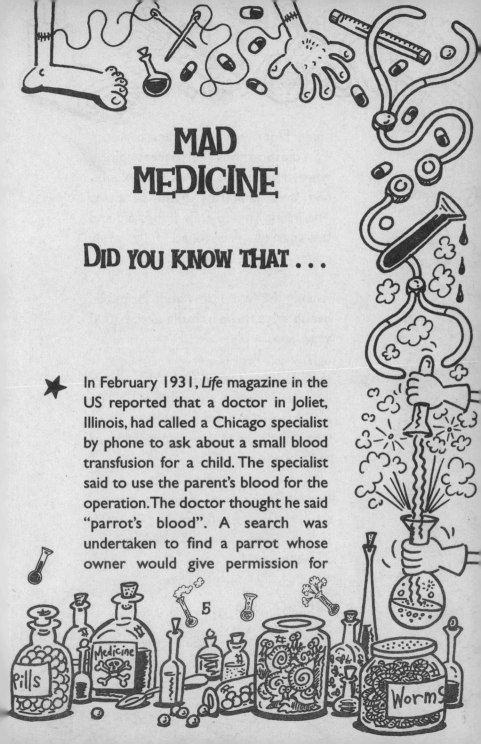

MAD
MEDICINE

DID YOU KNOW THAT ...

★ In February 1931, *Life* magazine in the US reported that a doctor in Joliet, Illinois, had called a Chicago specialist by phone to ask about a small blood transfusion for a child. The specialist said to use the parent's blood for the operation. The doctor thought he said "parrot's blood". A search was undertaken to find a parrot whose owner would give permission for

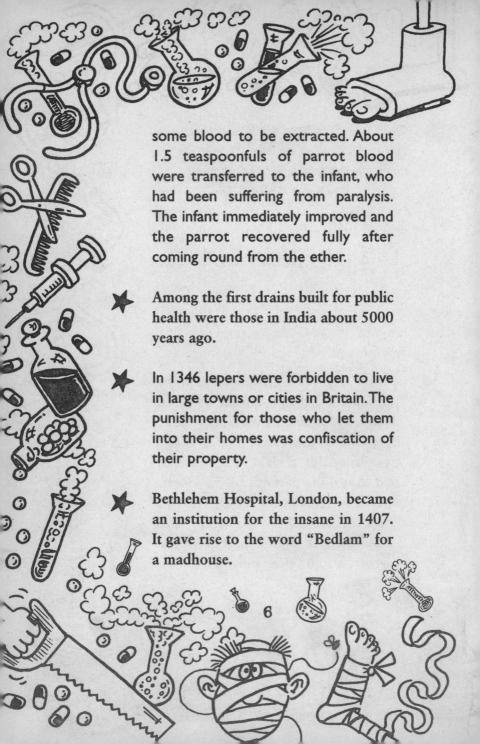

some blood to be extracted. About 1.5 teaspoonfuls of parrot blood were transferred to the infant, who had been suffering from paralysis. The infant immediately improved and the parrot recovered fully after coming round from the ether.

★ Among the first drains built for public health were those in India about 5000 years ago.

★ In 1346 lepers were forbidden to live in large towns or cities in Britain. The punishment for those who let them into their homes was confiscation of their property.

★ Bethlehem Hospital, London, became an institution for the insane in 1407. It gave rise to the word "Bedlam" for a madhouse.

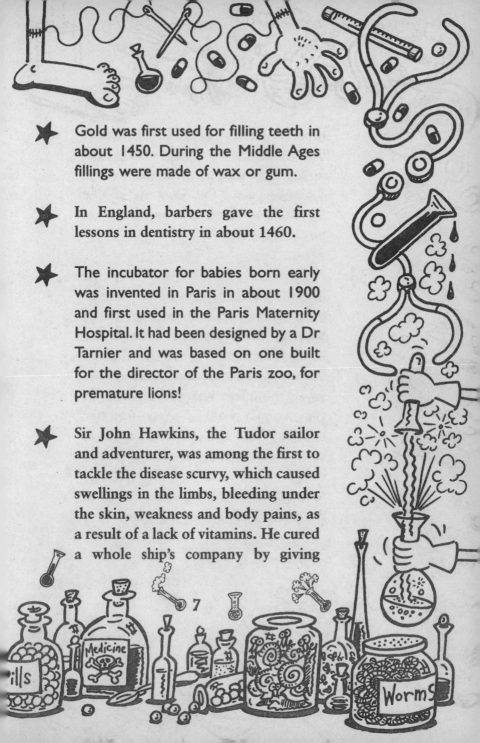

★ Gold was first used for filling teeth in about 1450. During the Middle Ages fillings were made of wax or gum.

★ In England, barbers gave the first lessons in dentistry in about 1460.

★ The incubator for babies born early was invented in Paris in about 1900 and first used in the Paris Maternity Hospital. It had been designed by a Dr Tarnier and was based on one built for the director of the Paris zoo, for premature lions!

★ Sir John Hawkins, the Tudor sailor and adventurer, was among the first to tackle the disease scurvy, which caused swellings in the limbs, bleeding under the skin, weakness and body pains, as a result of a lack of vitamins. He cured a whole ship's company by giving

7

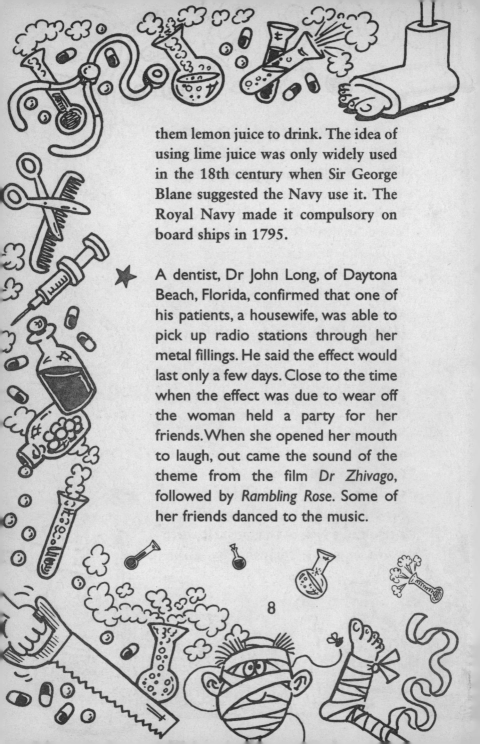

them lemon juice to drink. The idea of using lime juice was only widely used in the 18th century when Sir George Blane suggested the Navy use it. The Royal Navy made it compulsory on board ships in 1795.

A dentist, Dr John Long, of Daytona Beach, Florida, confirmed that one of his patients, a housewife, was able to pick up radio stations through her metal fillings. He said the effect would last only a few days. Close to the time when the effect was due to wear off the woman held a party for her friends. When she opened her mouth to laugh, out came the sound of the theme from the film *Dr Zhivago*, followed by *Rambling Rose*. Some of her friends danced to the music.

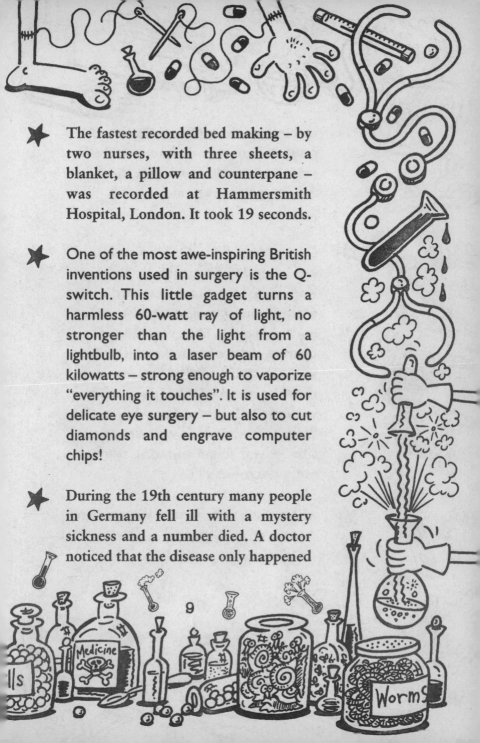

★ The fastest recorded bed making – by two nurses, with three sheets, a blanket, a pillow and counterpane – was recorded at Hammersmith Hospital, London. It took 19 seconds.

★ One of the most awe-inspiring British inventions used in surgery is the Q-switch. This little gadget turns a harmless 60-watt ray of light, no stronger than the light from a lightbulb, into a laser beam of 60 kilowatts – strong enough to vaporize "everything it touches". It is used for delicate eye surgery – but also to cut diamonds and engrave computer chips!

★ During the 19th century many people in Germany fell ill with a mystery sickness and a number died. A doctor noticed that the disease only happened

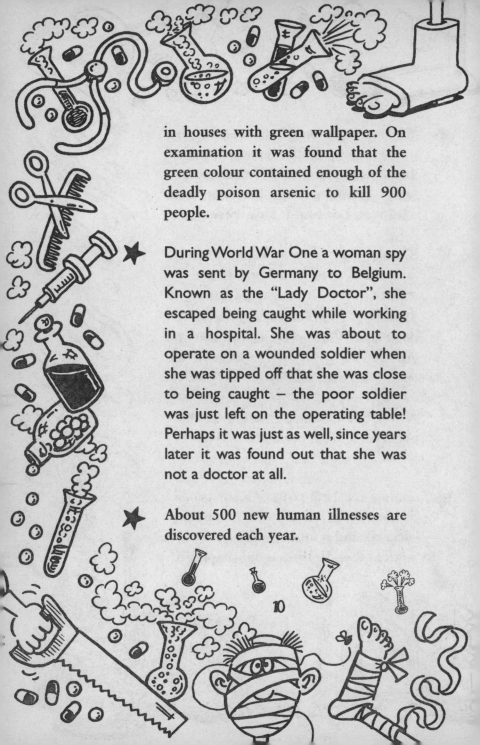

in houses with green wallpaper. On examination it was found that the green colour contained enough of the deadly poison arsenic to kill 900 people.

During World War One a woman spy was sent by Germany to Belgium. Known as the "Lady Doctor", she escaped being caught while working in a hospital. She was about to operate on a wounded soldier when she was tipped off that she was close to being caught — the poor soldier was just left on the operating table! Perhaps it was just as well, since years later it was found out that she was not a doctor at all.

About 500 new human illnesses are discovered each year.

10

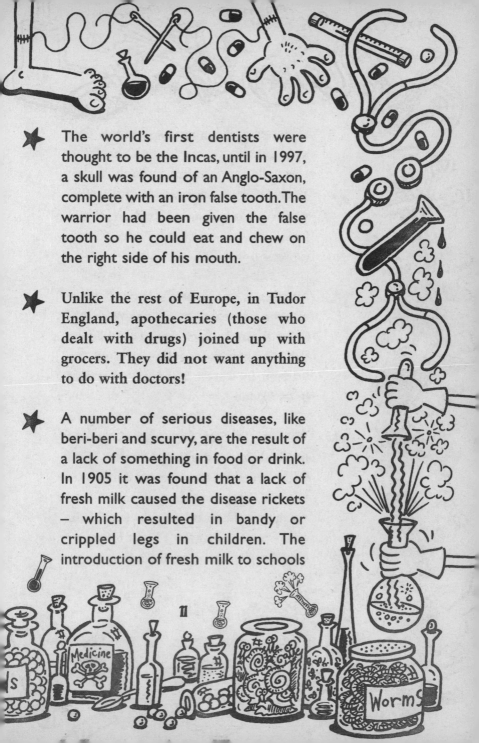

★ The world's first dentists were thought to be the Incas, until in 1997, a skull was found of an Anglo-Saxon, complete with an iron false tooth. The warrior had been given the false tooth so he could eat and chew on the right side of his mouth.

★ Unlike the rest of Europe, in Tudor England, apothecaries (those who dealt with drugs) joined up with grocers. They did not want anything to do with doctors!

★ A number of serious diseases, like beri-beri and scurvy, are the result of a lack of something in food or drink. In 1905 it was found that a lack of fresh milk caused the disease rickets — which resulted in bandy or crippled legs in children. The introduction of fresh milk to schools

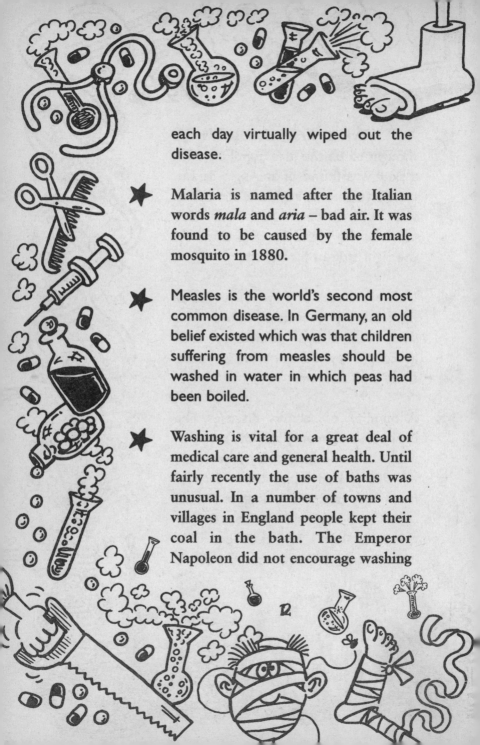

each day virtually wiped out the disease.

★ Malaria is named after the Italian words *mala* and *aria* – bad air. It was found to be caused by the female mosquito in 1880.

★ Measles is the world's second most common disease. In Germany, an old belief existed which was that children suffering from measles should be washed in water in which peas had been boiled.

★ Washing is vital for a great deal of medical care and general health. Until fairly recently the use of baths was unusual. In a number of towns and villages in England people kept their coal in the bath. The Emperor Napoleon did not encourage washing

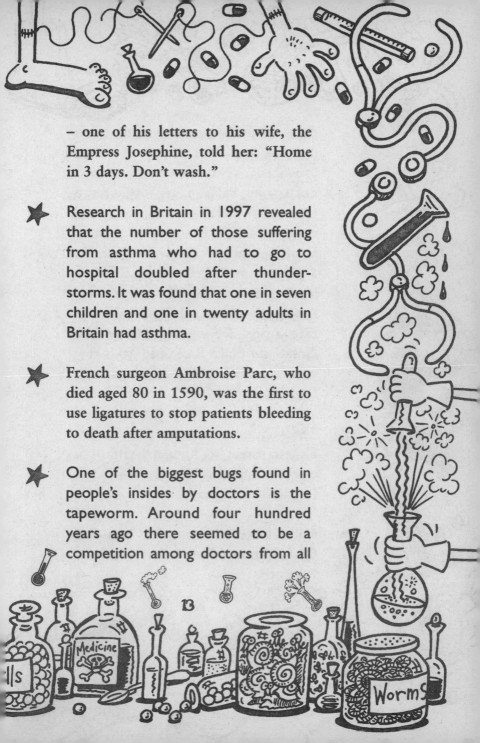

– one of his letters to his wife, the Empress Josephine, told her: "Home in 3 days. Don't wash."

★ Research in Britain in 1997 revealed that the number of those suffering from asthma who had to go to hospital doubled after thunderstorms. It was found that one in seven children and one in twenty adults in Britain had asthma.

★ French surgeon Ambroise Parc, who died aged 80 in 1590, was the first to use ligatures to stop patients bleeding to death after amputations.

★ One of the biggest bugs found in people's insides by doctors is the tapeworm. Around four hundred years ago there seemed to be a competition among doctors from all

13

parts of Europe to see who could find the largest. A doctor in Vienna produced a seven-metre one – then a doctor in Paris came up with a tapeworm 34.5 metres long and weighing a kilo! But they all seemed to be beaten by a tapeworm found in a peasant in St Petersburg, Russia – his was said to be 72 metres long! Among the famous people who had tapeworms were King Herod the Great and Philip II of Spain (the king who launched the Armada against England).

★ The common housefly may be the biggest threat to human health – it carries 30 different diseases which can be passed to humans.

★ Eight British monarchs, including Queen Anne, suffered from gout.

14

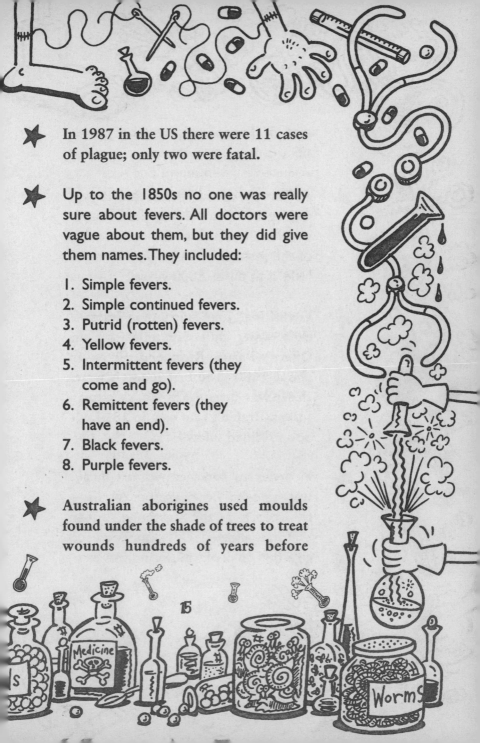

★ In 1987 in the US there were 11 cases of plague; only two were fatal.

★ Up to the 1850s no one was really sure about fevers. All doctors were vague about them, but they did give them names. They included:

1. Simple fevers.
2. Simple continued fevers.
3. Putrid (rotten) fevers.
4. Yellow fevers.
5. Intermittent fevers (they come and go).
6. Remittent fevers (they have an end).
7. Black fevers.
8. Purple fevers.

★ Australian aborigines used moulds found under the shade of trees to treat wounds hundreds of years before

15

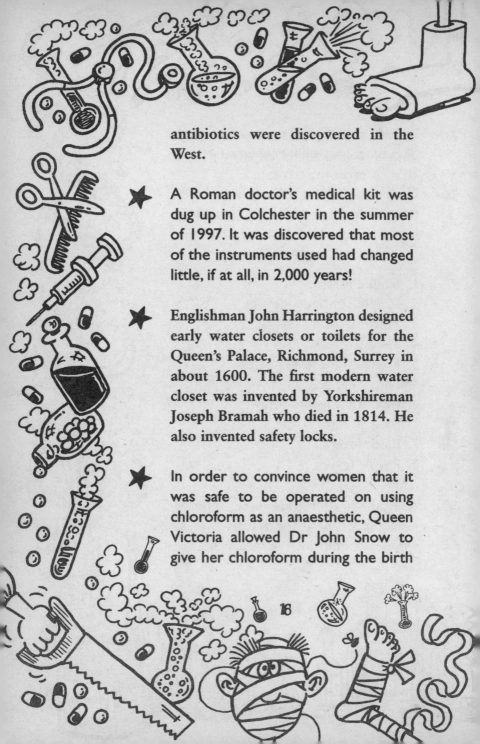

antibiotics were discovered in the West.

★ A Roman doctor's medical kit was dug up in Colchester in the summer of 1997. It was discovered that most of the instruments used had changed little, if at all, in 2,000 years!

★ Englishman John Harrington designed early water closets or toilets for the Queen's Palace, Richmond, Surrey in about 1600. The first modern water closet was invented by Yorkshireman Joseph Bramah who died in 1814. He also invented safety locks.

★ In order to convince women that it was safe to be operated on using chloroform as an anaesthetic, Queen Victoria allowed Dr John Snow to give her chloroform during the birth

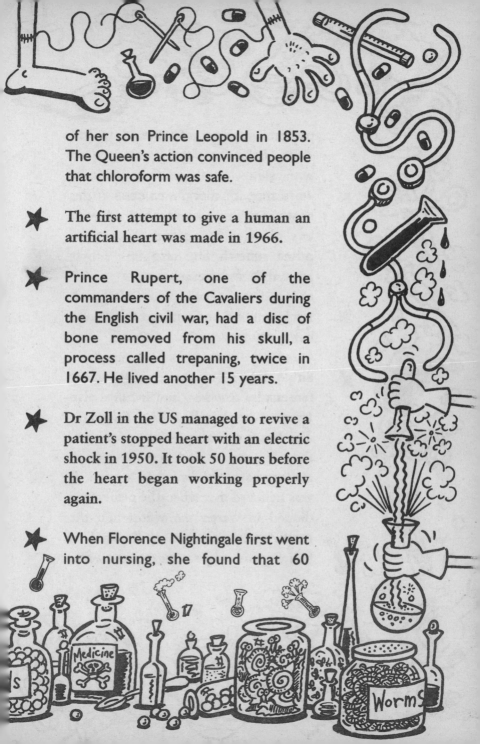

of her son Prince Leopold in 1853. The Queen's action convinced people that chloroform was safe.

★ The first attempt to give a human an artificial heart was made in 1966.

★ Prince Rupert, one of the commanders of the Cavaliers during the English civil war, had a disc of bone removed from his skull, a process called trepaning, twice in 1667. He lived another 15 years.

★ Dr Zoll in the US managed to revive a patient's stopped heart with an electric shock in 1950. It took 50 hours before the heart began working properly again.

★ When Florence Nightingale first went into nursing, she found that 60

17

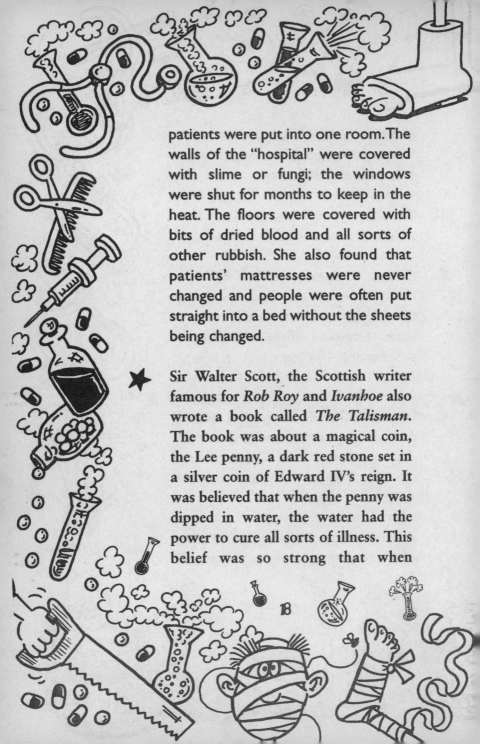

patients were put into one room. The walls of the "hospital" were covered with slime or fungi; the windows were shut for months to keep in the heat. The floors were covered with bits of dried blood and all sorts of other rubbish. She also found that patients' mattresses were never changed and people were often put straight into a bed without the sheets being changed.

Sir Walter Scott, the Scottish writer famous for *Rob Roy* and *Ivanhoe* also wrote a book called *The Talisman*. The book was about a magical coin, the Lee penny, a dark red stone set in a silver coin of Edward IV's reign. It was believed that when the penny was dipped in water, the water had the power to cure all sorts of illness. This belief was so strong that when

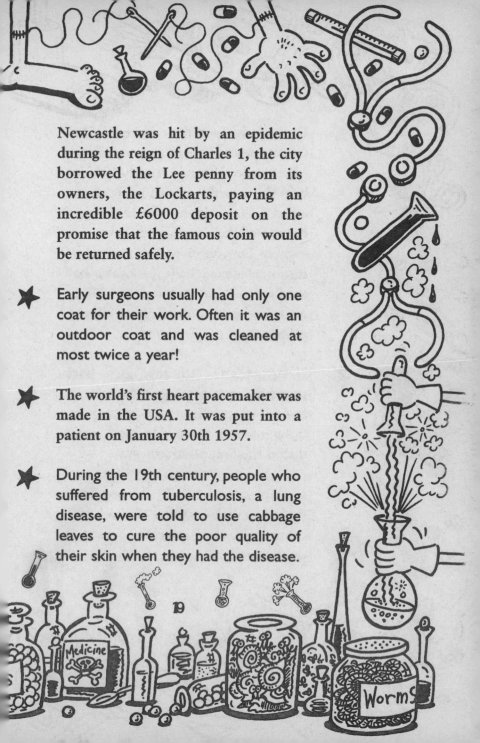

Newcastle was hit by an epidemic during the reign of Charles 1, the city borrowed the Lee penny from its owners, the Lockarts, paying an incredible £6000 deposit on the promise that the famous coin would be returned safely.

★ Early surgeons usually had only one coat for their work. Often it was an outdoor coat and was cleaned at most twice a year!

★ The world's first heart pacemaker was made in the USA. It was put into a patient on January 30th 1957.

★ During the 19th century, people who suffered from tuberculosis, a lung disease, were told to use cabbage leaves to cure the poor quality of their skin when they had the disease.

Medicine

Worms

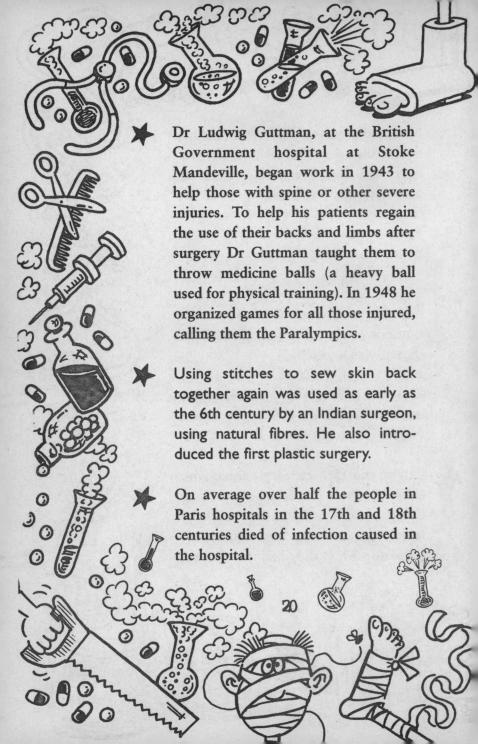

★ Dr Ludwig Guttman, at the British Government hospital at Stoke Mandeville, began work in 1943 to help those with spine or other severe injuries. To help his patients regain the use of their backs and limbs after surgery Dr Guttman taught them to throw medicine balls (a heavy ball used for physical training). In 1948 he organized games for all those injured, calling them the Paralympics.

★ Using stitches to sew skin back together again was used as early as the 6th century by an Indian surgeon, using natural fibres. He also introduced the first plastic surgery.

★ On average over half the people in Paris hospitals in the 17th and 18th centuries died of infection caused in the hospital.

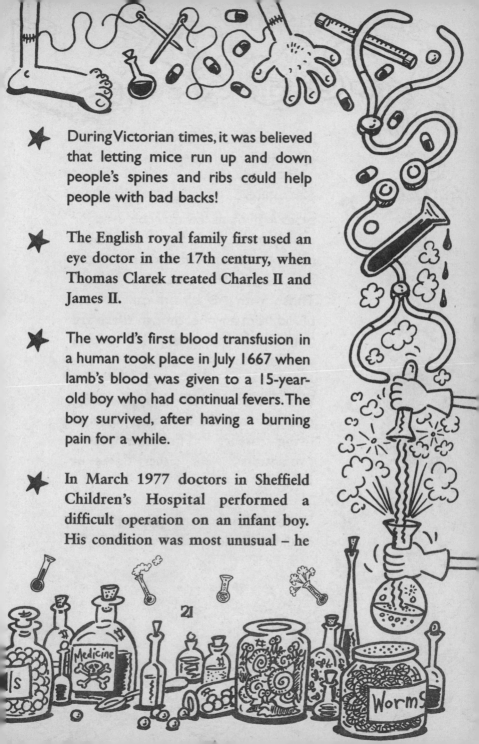

★ During Victorian times, it was believed that letting mice run up and down people's spines and ribs could help people with bad backs!

★ The English royal family first used an eye doctor in the 17th century, when Thomas Clarek treated Charles II and James II.

★ The world's first blood transfusion in a human took place in July 1667 when lamb's blood was given to a 15-year-old boy who had continual fevers. The boy survived, after having a burning pain for a while.

★ In March 1977 doctors in Sheffield Children's Hospital performed a difficult operation on an infant boy. His condition was most unusual – he

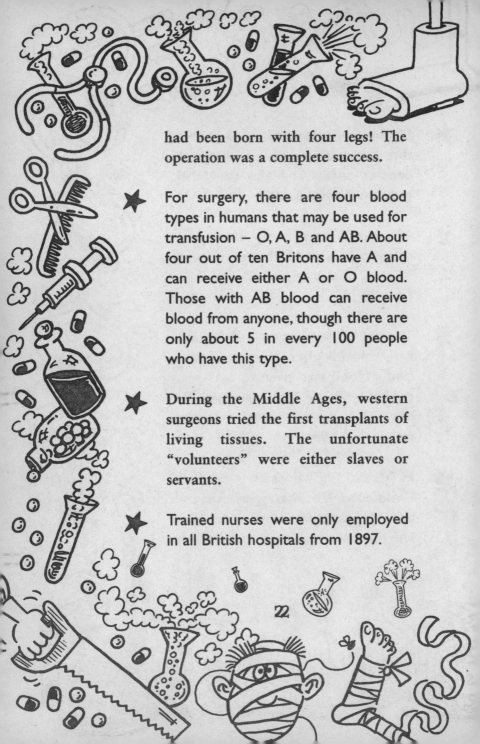

had been born with four legs! The operation was a complete success.

★ For surgery, there are four blood types in humans that may be used for transfusion – O, A, B and AB. About four out of ten Britons have A and can receive either A or O blood. Those with AB blood can receive blood from anyone, though there are only about 5 in every 100 people who have this type.

★ During the Middle Ages, western surgeons tried the first transplants of living tissues. The unfortunate "volunteers" were either slaves or servants.

★ Trained nurses were only employed in all British hospitals from 1897.

22

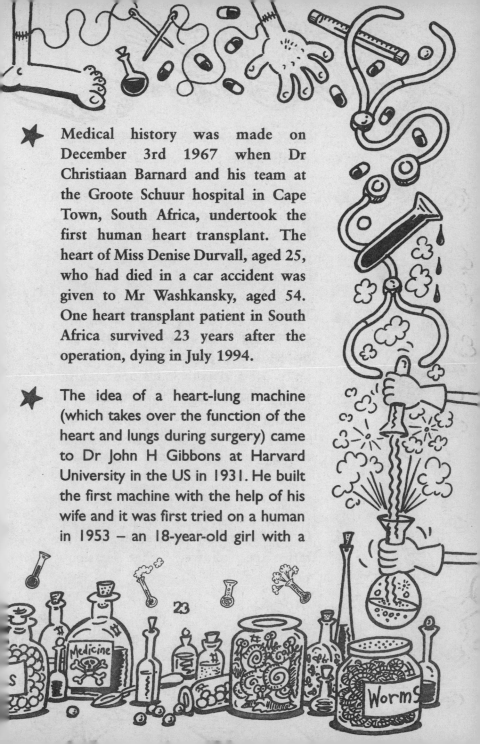

★ Medical history was made on December 3rd 1967 when Dr Christiaan Barnard and his team at the Groote Schuur hospital in Cape Town, South Africa, undertook the first human heart transplant. The heart of Miss Denise Durvall, aged 25, who had died in a car accident was given to Mr Washkansky, aged 54. One heart transplant patient in South Africa survived 23 years after the operation, dying in July 1994.

★ The idea of a heart-lung machine (which takes over the function of the heart and lungs during surgery) came to Dr John H Gibbons at Harvard University in the US in 1931. He built the first machine with the help of his wife and it was first tried on a human in 1953 — an 18-year-old girl with a

23

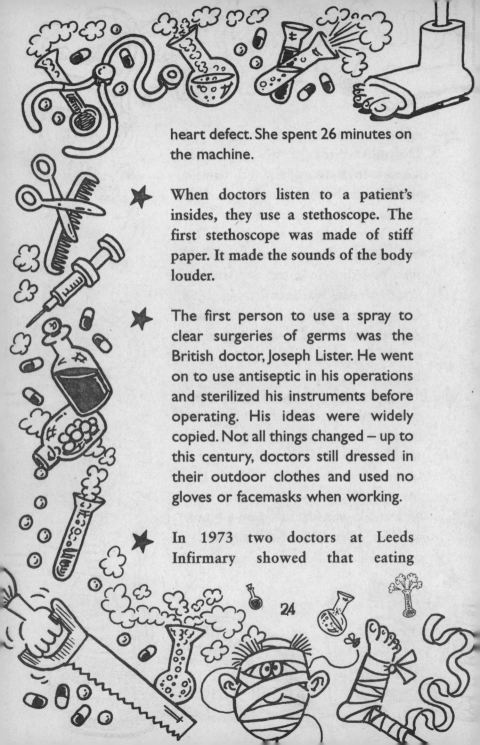

heart defect. She spent 26 minutes on the machine.

★ When doctors listen to a patient's insides, they use a stethoscope. The first stethoscope was made of stiff paper. It made the sounds of the body louder.

★ The first person to use a spray to clear surgeries of germs was the British doctor, Joseph Lister. He went on to use antiseptic in his operations and sterilized his instruments before operating. His ideas were widely copied. Not all things changed – up to this century, doctors still dressed in their outdoor clothes and used no gloves or facemasks when working.

★ In 1973 two doctors at Leeds Infirmary showed that eating

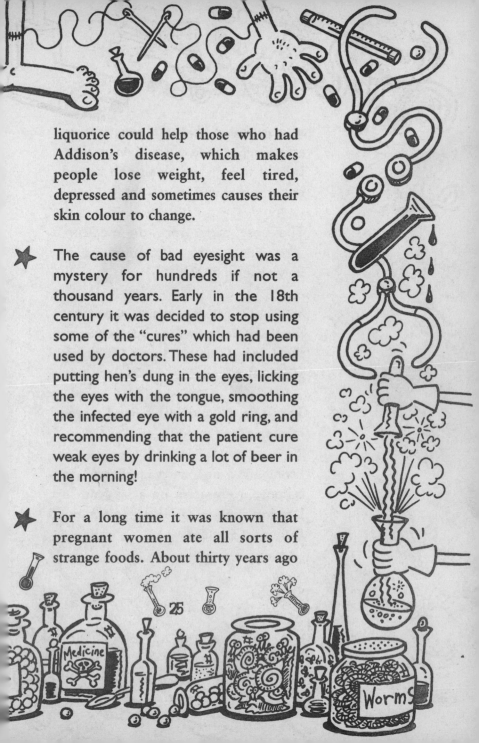

liquorice could help those who had Addison's disease, which makes people lose weight, feel tired, depressed and sometimes causes their skin colour to change.

★ The cause of bad eyesight was a mystery for hundreds if not a thousand years. Early in the 18th century it was decided to stop using some of the "cures" which had been used by doctors. These had included putting hen's dung in the eyes, licking the eyes with the tongue, smoothing the infected eye with a gold ring, and recommending that the patient cure weak eyes by drinking a lot of beer in the morning!

★ For a long time it was known that pregnant women ate all sorts of strange foods. About thirty years ago

25

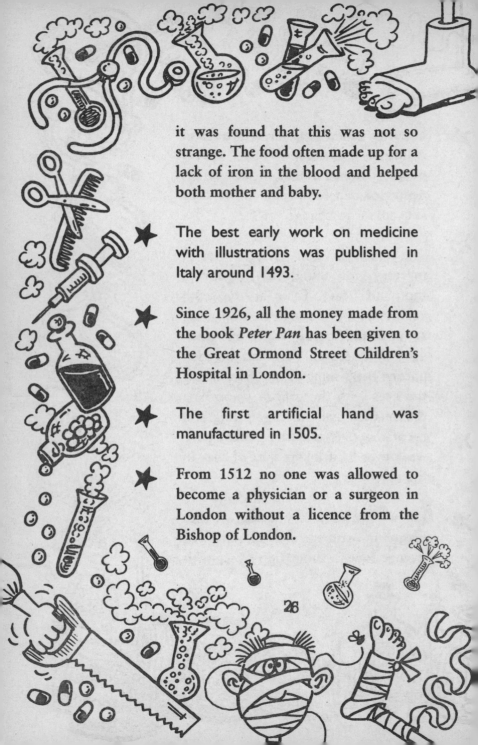

it was found that this was not so strange. The food often made up for a lack of iron in the blood and helped both mother and baby.

The best early work on medicine with illustrations was published in Italy around 1493.

Since 1926, all the money made from the book *Peter Pan* has been given to the Great Ormond Street Children's Hospital in London.

The first artificial hand was manufactured in 1505.

From 1512 no one was allowed to become a physician or a surgeon in London without a licence from the Bishop of London.

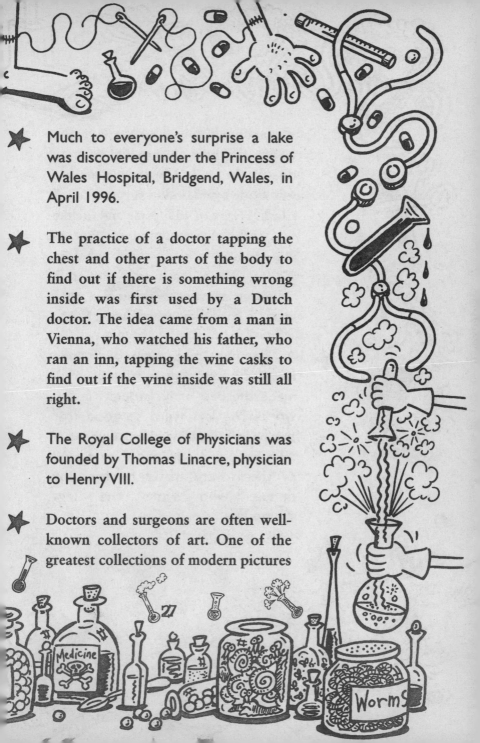

★ Much to everyone's surprise a lake was discovered under the Princess of Wales Hospital, Bridgend, Wales, in April 1996.

★ The practice of a doctor tapping the chest and other parts of the body to find out if there is something wrong inside was first used by a Dutch doctor. The idea came from a man in Vienna, who watched his father, who ran an inn, tapping the wine casks to find out if the wine inside was still all right.

★ The Royal College of Physicians was founded by Thomas Linacre, physician to Henry VIII.

★ Doctors and surgeons are often well-known collectors of art. One of the greatest collections of modern pictures

27

was put together by a Dr Barnes in the USA and is now on show. In England one of the most unusual collections was made by a London surgeon called Clark. He had 140 lifesize and lifelike waxworks of kings, emperors, queens and princes in their royal robes in 1760. What happened to this collection remains a mystery – they seem to have disappeared after 1831.

★ A German man named Striede founded a workshop in Austria which made the best artificial limbs in the world. The legs were so good that the people wearing them could run upstairs, play tennis and even ski. All of them were made by hand by people who wore the legs themselves.

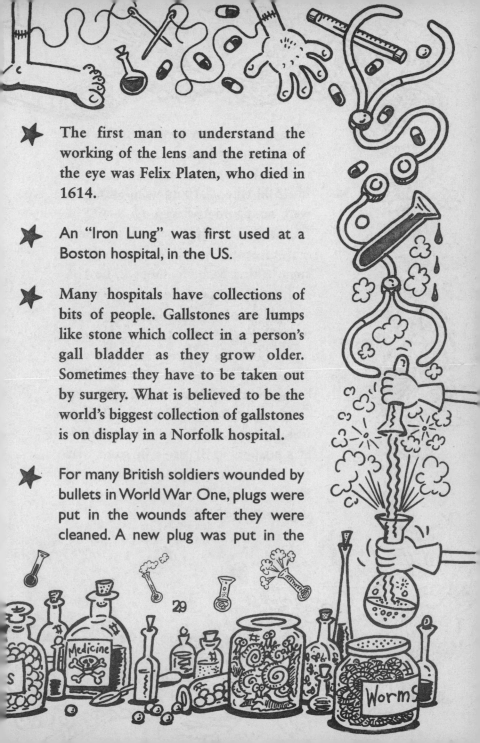

★ The first man to understand the working of the lens and the retina of the eye was Felix Platen, who died in 1614.

★ An "Iron Lung" was first used at a Boston hospital, in the US.

★ Many hospitals have collections of bits of people. Gallstones are lumps like stone which collect in a person's gall bladder as they grow older. Sometimes they have to be taken out by surgery. What is believed to be the world's biggest collection of gallstones is on display in a Norfolk hospital.

★ For many British soldiers wounded by bullets in World War One, plugs were put in the wounds after they were cleaned. A new plug was put in the hole about once a week until the wound was healed.

★ In 1504 the Barbers and Surgeons were amalgamated into one Guild in England. The link between barbers and surgeons is still remembered in some older barber's shops. The red and white pole used as a sign is symbolic of a bandage wrapped around an arm prior to blood letting.

★ The world's first blood transfusion using human blood took place at Guy's Hospital, London, in 1818. It was, however, not until March 1917, at a hospital in Brussels, Belgium, that the first successful transfusion of blood from one human to another was achieved.

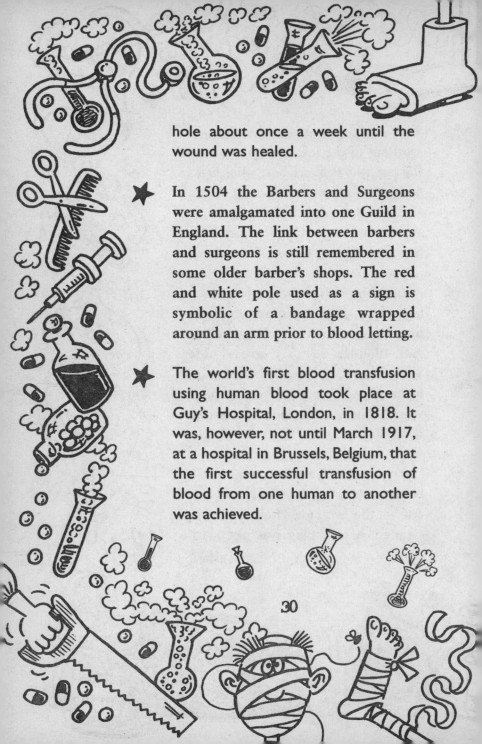

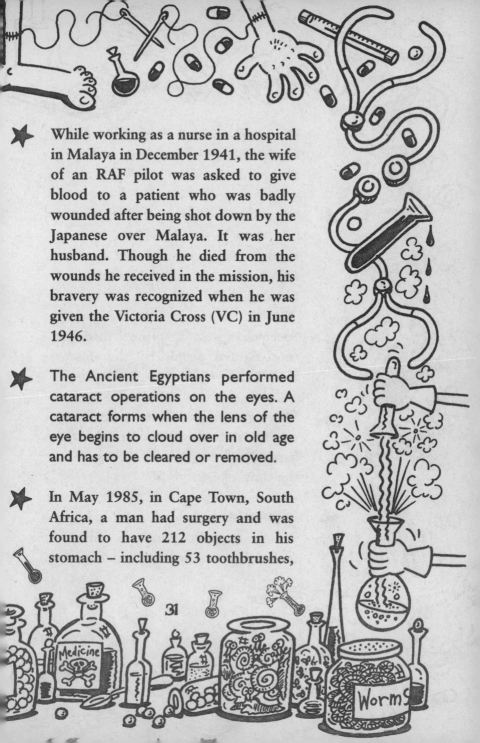

While working as a nurse in a hospital in Malaya in December 1941, the wife of an RAF pilot was asked to give blood to a patient who was badly wounded after being shot down by the Japanese over Malaya. It was her husband. Though he died from the wounds he received in the mission, his bravery was recognized when he was given the Victoria Cross (VC) in June 1946.

The Ancient Egyptians performed cataract operations on the eyes. A cataract forms when the lens of the eye begins to cloud over in old age and has to be cleared or removed.

In May 1985, in Cape Town, South Africa, a man had surgery and was found to have 212 objects in his stomach – including 53 toothbrushes,

31

two telescopic aerials, two razor heads with blades and 150 handles of disposable razors!

★ In ancient Persia, the tears of mourners were saved and put in bottles. They were believed to have the power to cure a number of diseases.

★ Spectacles were first prescribed for short-sighted people by the doctor Hollerius in 1550.

★ Three generations of the same family were eye doctors to the British royal family from the time of George II to the time of George IV.

★ In the 19th century a Dr Dill in Hong Kong suggested that the disease malaria was caused by "exposure to

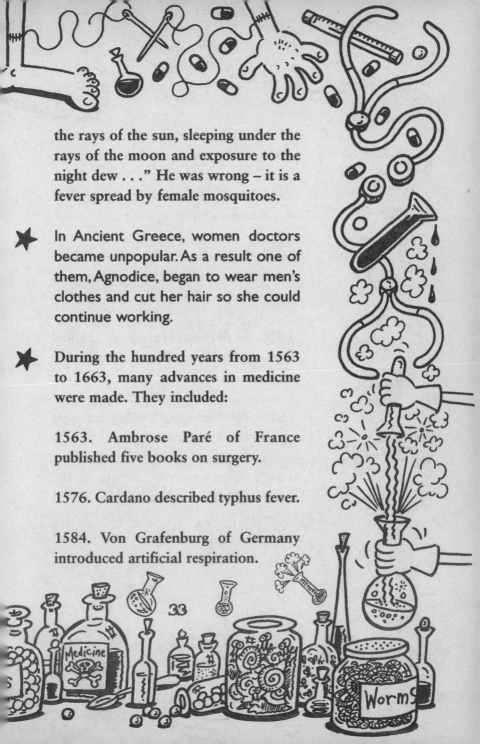

the rays of the sun, sleeping under the rays of the moon and exposure to the night dew . . ." He was wrong – it is a fever spread by female mosquitoes.

★ In Ancient Greece, women doctors became unpopular. As a result one of them, Agnodice, began to wear men's clothes and cut her hair so she could continue working.

★ During the hundred years from 1563 to 1663, many advances in medicine were made. They included:

1563. Ambrose Paré of France published five books on surgery.

1576. Cardano described typhus fever.

1584. Von Grafenburg of Germany introduced artificial respiration.

33

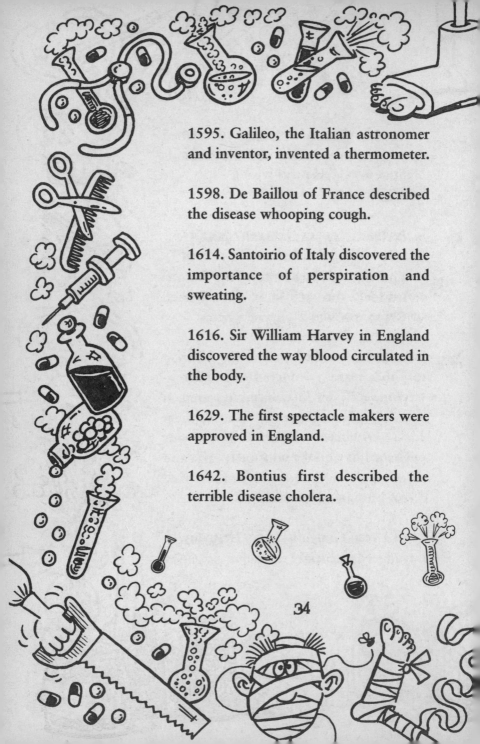

1595. Galileo, the Italian astronomer and inventor, invented a thermometer.

1598. De Baillou of France described the disease whooping cough.

1614. Santoirio of Italy discovered the importance of perspiration and sweating.

1616. Sir William Harvey in England discovered the way blood circulated in the body.

1629. The first spectacle makers were approved in England.

1642. Bontius first described the terrible disease cholera.

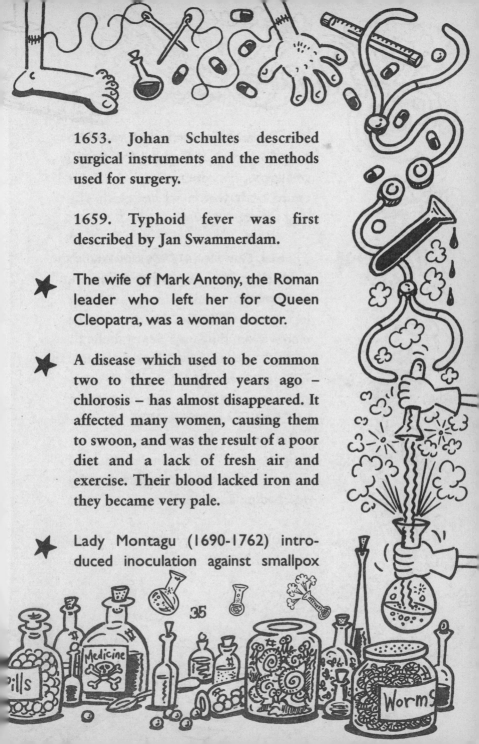

1653. Johan Schultes described surgical instruments and the methods used for surgery.

1659. Typhoid fever was first described by Jan Swammerdam.

★ The wife of Mark Antony, the Roman leader who left her for Queen Cleopatra, was a woman doctor.

★ A disease which used to be common two to three hundred years ago – chlorosis – has almost disappeared. It affected many women, causing them to swoon, and was the result of a poor diet and a lack of fresh air and exercise. Their blood lacked iron and they became very pale.

★ Lady Montagu (1690-1762) introduced inoculation against smallpox

35

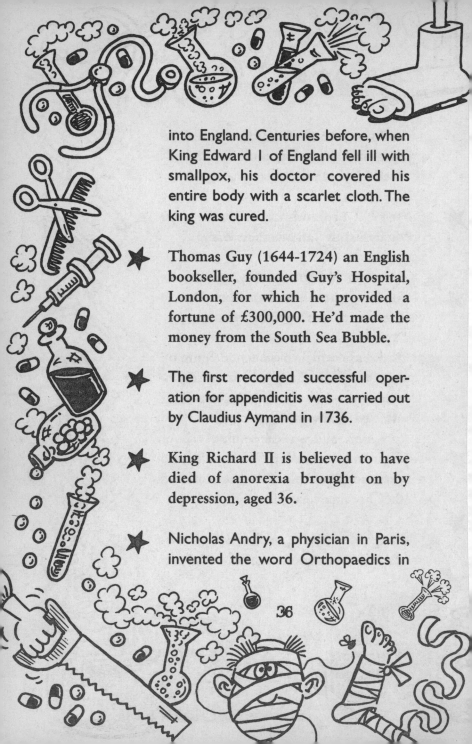

into England. Centuries before, when King Edward 1 of England fell ill with smallpox, his doctor covered his entire body with a scarlet cloth. The king was cured.

★ Thomas Guy (1644-1724) an English bookseller, founded Guy's Hospital, London, for which he provided a fortune of £300,000. He'd made the money from the South Sea Bubble.

★ The first recorded successful operation for appendicitis was carried out by Claudius Aymand in 1736.

★ King Richard II is believed to have died of anorexia brought on by depression, aged 36.

★ Nicholas Andry, a physician in Paris, invented the word Orthopaedics in

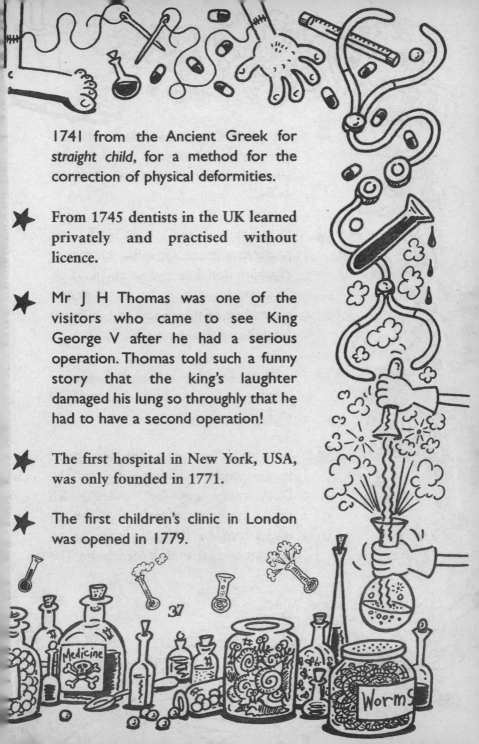

1741 from the Ancient Greek for *straight child*, for a method for the correction of physical deformities.

★ From 1745 dentists in the UK learned privately and practised without licence.

★ Mr J H Thomas was one of the visitors who came to see King George V after he had a serious operation. Thomas told such a funny story that the king's laughter damaged his lung so throughly that he had to have a second operation!

★ The first hospital in New York, USA, was only founded in 1771.

★ The first children's clinic in London was opened in 1779.

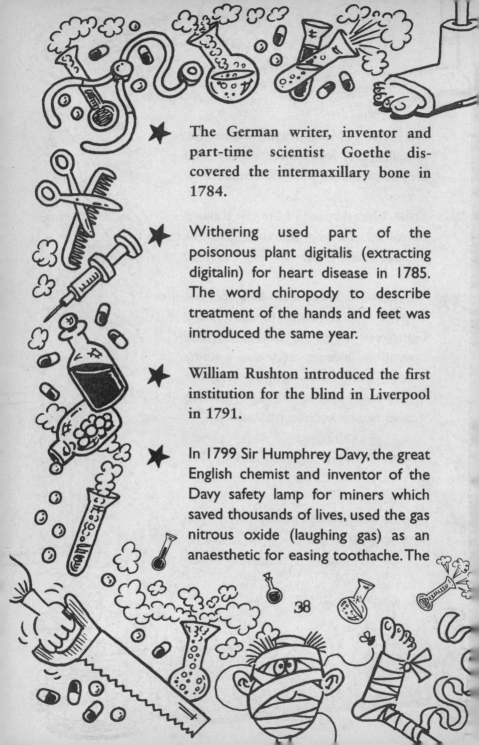

★ The German writer, inventor and part-time scientist Goethe discovered the intermaxillary bone in 1784.

★ Withering used part of the poisonous plant digitalis (extracting digitalin) for heart disease in 1785. The word chiropody to describe treatment of the hands and feet was introduced the same year.

★ William Rushton introduced the first institution for the blind in Liverpool in 1791.

★ In 1799 Sir Humphrey Davy, the great English chemist and inventor of the Davy safety lamp for miners which saved thousands of lives, used the gas nitrous oxide (laughing gas) as an anaesthetic for easing toothache. The

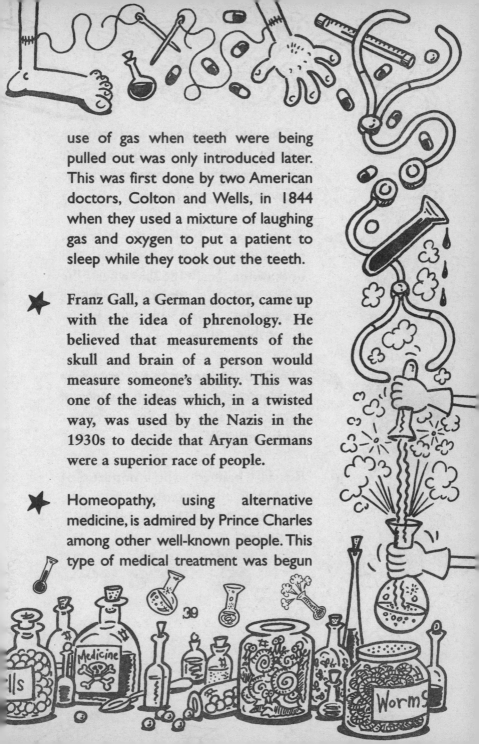

use of gas when teeth were being pulled out was only introduced later. This was first done by two American doctors, Colton and Wells, in 1844 when they used a mixture of laughing gas and oxygen to put a patient to sleep while they took out the teeth.

★ Franz Gall, a German doctor, came up with the idea of phrenology. He believed that measurements of the skull and brain of a person would measure someone's ability. This was one of the ideas which, in a twisted way, was used by the Nazis in the 1930s to decide that Aryan Germans were a superior race of people.

★ Homeopathy, using alternative medicine, is admired by Prince Charles among other well-known people. This type of medical treatment was begun

39

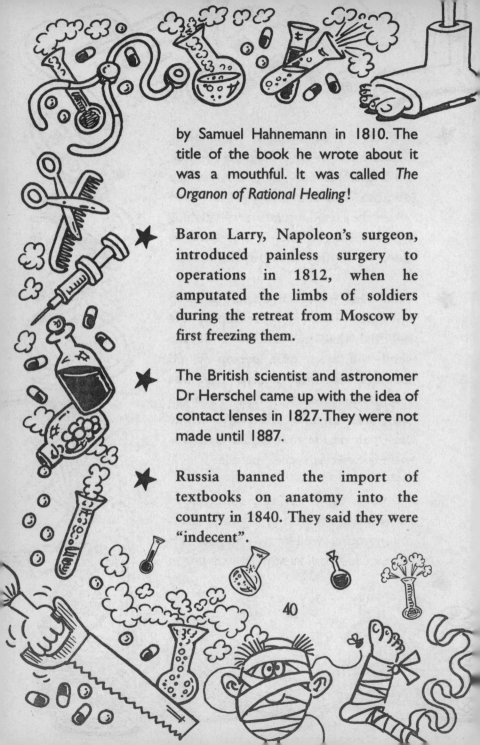

by Samuel Hahnemann in 1810. The title of the book he wrote about it was a mouthful. It was called *The Organon of Rational Healing*!

★ Baron Larry, Napoleon's surgeon, introduced painless surgery to operations in 1812, when he amputated the limbs of soldiers during the retreat from Moscow by first freezing them.

★ The British scientist and astronomer Dr Herschel came up with the idea of contact lenses in 1827. They were not made until 1887.

★ Russia banned the import of textbooks on anatomy into the country in 1840. They said they were "indecent".

40

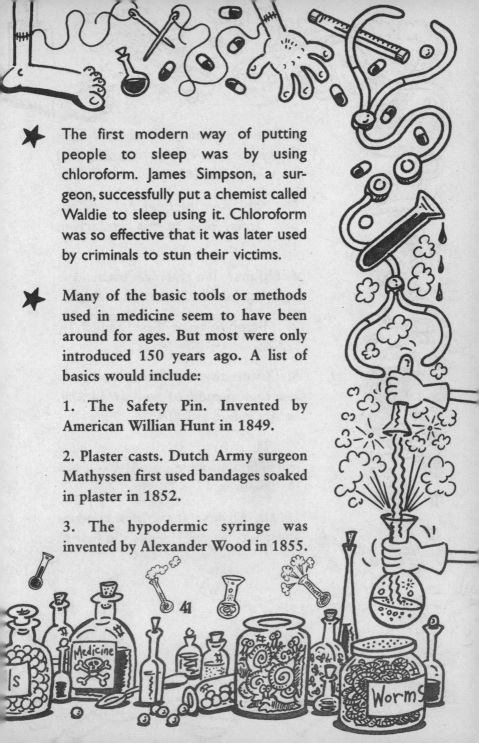

The first modern way of putting people to sleep was by using chloroform. James Simpson, a surgeon, successfully put a chemist called Waldie to sleep using it. Chloroform was so effective that it was later used by criminals to stun their victims.

Many of the basic tools or methods used in medicine seem to have been around for ages. But most were only introduced 150 years ago. A list of basics would include:

1. The Safety Pin. Invented by American Willian Hunt in 1849.

2. Plaster casts. Dutch Army surgeon Mathyssen first used bandages soaked in plaster in 1852.

3. The hypodermic syringe was invented by Alexander Wood in 1855.

Medicine

Is

Worms

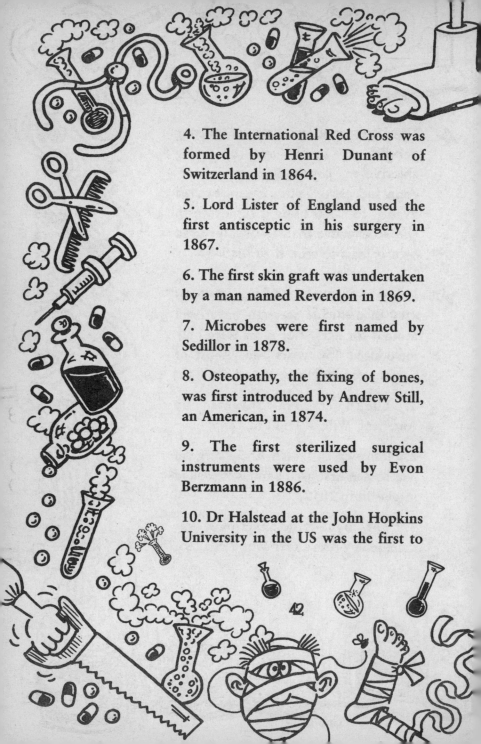

4. The International Red Cross was formed by Henri Dunant of Switzerland in 1864.

5. Lord Lister of England used the first antisceptic in his surgery in 1867.

6. The first skin graft was undertaken by a man named Reverdon in 1869.

7. Microbes were first named by Sedillor in 1878.

8. Osteopathy, the fixing of bones, was first introduced by Andrew Still, an American, in 1874.

9. The first sterilized surgical instruments were used by Evon Berzmann in 1886.

10. Dr Halstead at the John Hopkins University in the US was the first to

use rubber gloves during surgery in 1890.

11. Aspirin was introduced by Herman Dresser in 1893.

12. Appendicitis was first discovered in 1886 by R H Fitz in the USA.

★ The patron saint for those with toothache is St Apollonia.

★ In 1818 France published an illustrated guide to hospitals in Paris – they had over 37,000 beds.

★ The Prince of Nassau, Germany, was persuaded by his doctor to take water treatments. Over the years he had 500 cold baths, 2,400 salt baths, spent 480 hours in wet sheets and drank 3,500 tumblers of cold water.

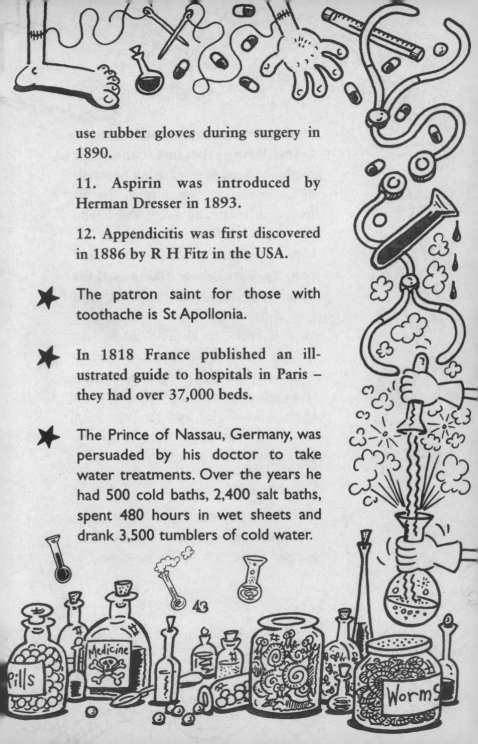

43

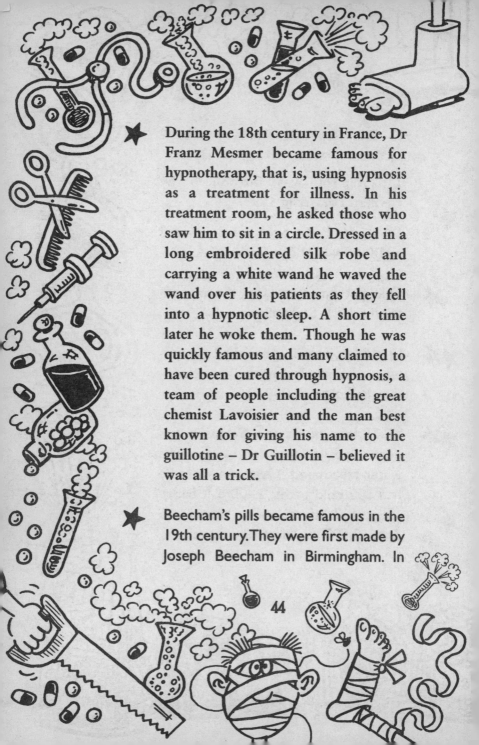

During the 18th century in France, Dr Franz Mesmer became famous for hypnotherapy, that is, using hypnosis as a treatment for illness. In his treatment room, he asked those who saw him to sit in a circle. Dressed in a long embroidered silk robe and carrying a white wand he waved the wand over his patients as they fell into a hypnotic sleep. A short time later he woke them. Though he was quickly famous and many claimed to have been cured through hypnosis, a team of people including the great chemist Lavoisier and the man best known for giving his name to the guillotine – Dr Guillotin – believed it was all a trick.

Beecham's pills became famous in the 19th century. They were first made by Joseph Beecham in Birmingham. In

44

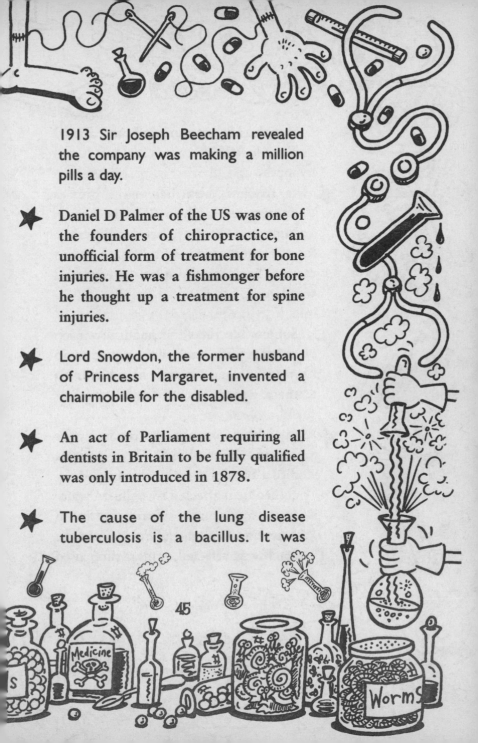

1913 Sir Joseph Beecham revealed the company was making a million pills a day.

★ Daniel D Palmer of the US was one of the founders of chiropractice, an unofficial form of treatment for bone injuries. He was a fishmonger before he thought up a treatment for spine injuries.

★ Lord Snowdon, the former husband of Princess Margaret, invented a chairmobile for the disabled.

★ An act of Parliament requiring all dentists in Britain to be fully qualified was only introduced in 1878.

★ The cause of the lung disease tuberculosis is a bacillus. It was

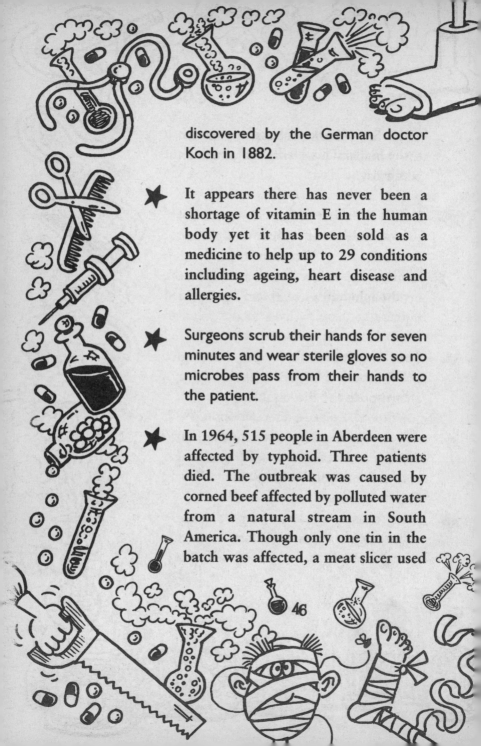

discovered by the German doctor Koch in 1882.

★ It appears there has never been a shortage of vitamin E in the human body yet it has been sold as a medicine to help up to 29 conditions including ageing, heart disease and allergies.

★ Surgeons scrub their hands for seven minutes and wear sterile gloves so no microbes pass from their hands to the patient.

★ In 1964, 515 people in Aberdeen were affected by typhoid. Three patients died. The outbreak was caused by corned beef affected by polluted water from a natural stream in South America. Though only one tin in the batch was affected, a meat slicer used

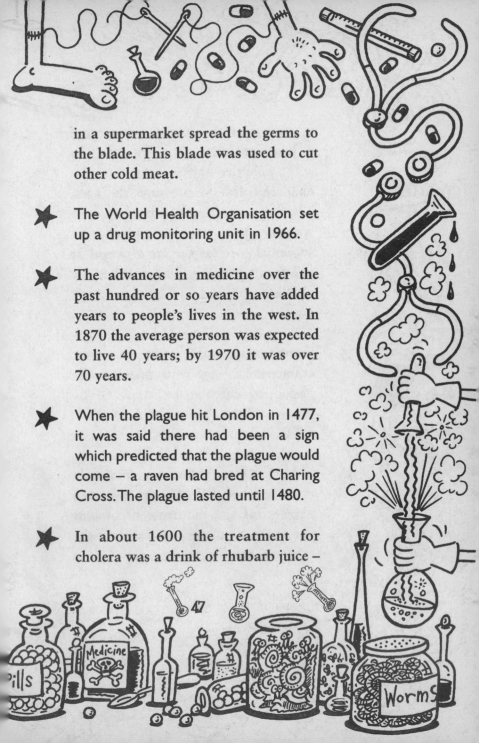

in a supermarket spread the germs to the blade. This blade was used to cut other cold meat.

★ The World Health Organisation set up a drug monitoring unit in 1966.

★ The advances in medicine over the past hundred or so years have added years to people's lives in the west. In 1870 the average person was expected to live 40 years; by 1970 it was over 70 years.

★ When the plague hit London in 1477, it was said there had been a sign which predicted that the plague would come – a raven had bred at Charing Cross. The plague lasted until 1480.

★ In about 1600 the treatment for cholera was a drink of rhubarb juice –

47

if you were rich – or rose hip syrup – if you were poor. Rose hip syrup is still available, having been used for children's illnesses through the ages. The best protection against the plague was thought to be onions, which were supposed to clear the air of germs in ten days. Overall, it was reckoned the ultimate cure was powdered unicorn's horn!

★ France and Italy were the first countries to try and prevent the plague by introducing rules to be followed if the illness struck, in about 1500.

★ In 1577, a vicar in London announced in a sermon that the cause of the plague was sin, the cause of sin was the acting of plays and therefore the cause of the plague was plays! As a

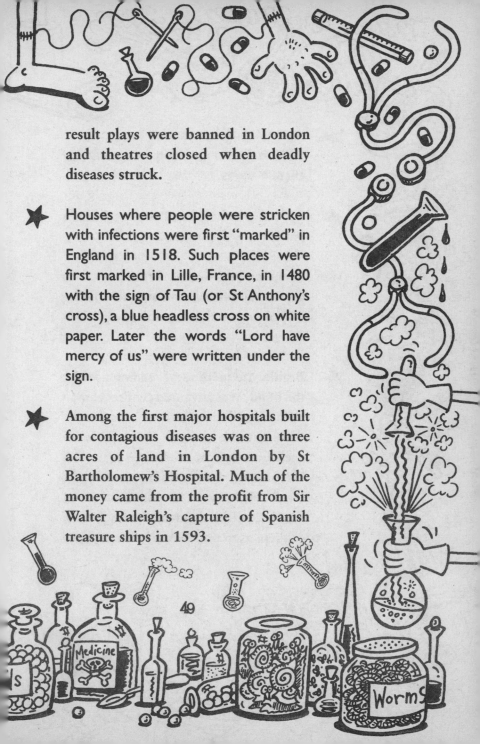

result plays were banned in London and theatres closed when deadly diseases struck.

★ Houses where people were stricken with infections were first "marked" in England in 1518. Such places were first marked in Lille, France, in 1480 with the sign of Tau (or St Anthony's cross), a blue headless cross on white paper. Later the words "Lord have mercy of us" were written under the sign.

★ Among the first major hospitals built for contagious diseases was on three acres of land in London by St Bartholomew's Hospital. Much of the money came from the profit from Sir Walter Raleigh's capture of Spanish treasure ships in 1593.

49

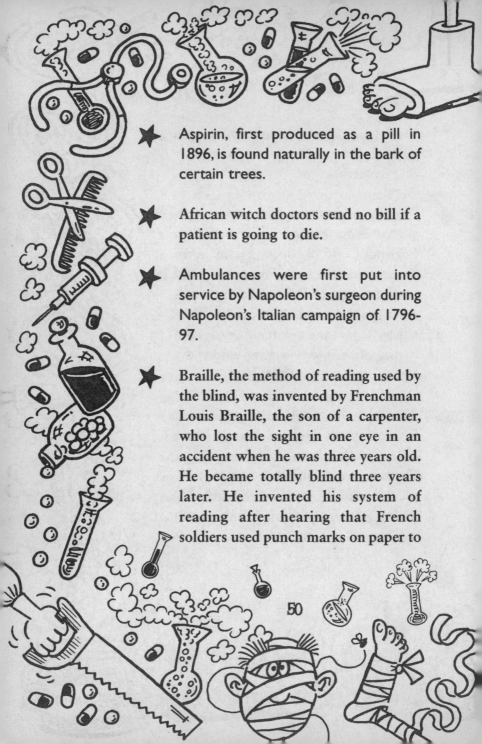

★ Aspirin, first produced as a pill in 1896, is found naturally in the bark of certain trees.

★ African witch doctors send no bill if a patient is going to die.

★ Ambulances were first put into service by Napoleon's surgeon during Napoleon's Italian campaign of 1796-97.

★ Braille, the method of reading used by the blind, was invented by Frenchman Louis Braille, the son of a carpenter, who lost the sight in one eye in an accident when he was three years old. He became totally blind three years later. He invented his system of reading after hearing that French soldiers used punch marks on paper to

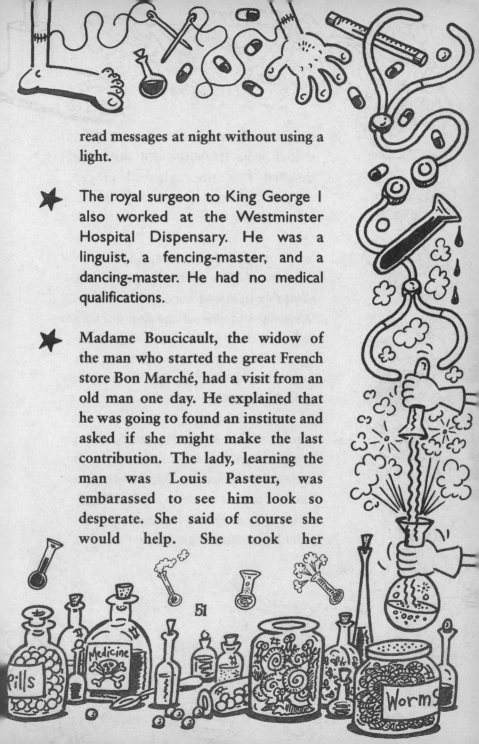

read messages at night without using a light.

★ The royal surgeon to King George I also worked at the Westminster Hospital Dispensary. He was a linguist, a fencing-master, and a dancing-master. He had no medical qualifications.

★ Madame Boucicault, the widow of the man who started the great French store Bon Marché, had a visit from an old man one day. He explained that he was going to found an institute and asked if she might make the last contribution. The lady, learning the man was Louis Pasteur, was embarassed to see him look so desperate. She said of course she would help. She took her

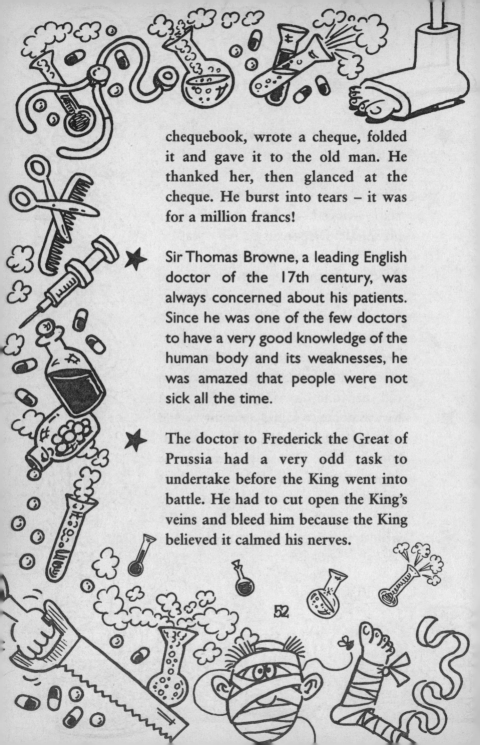

chequebook, wrote a cheque, folded it and gave it to the old man. He thanked her, then glanced at the cheque. He burst into tears – it was for a million francs!

Sir Thomas Browne, a leading English doctor of the 17th century, was always concerned about his patients. Since he was one of the few doctors to have a very good knowledge of the human body and its weaknesses, he was amazed that people were not sick all the time.

The doctor to Frederick the Great of Prussia had a very odd task to undertake before the King went into battle. He had to cut open the King's veins and bleed him because the King believed it calmed his nerves.

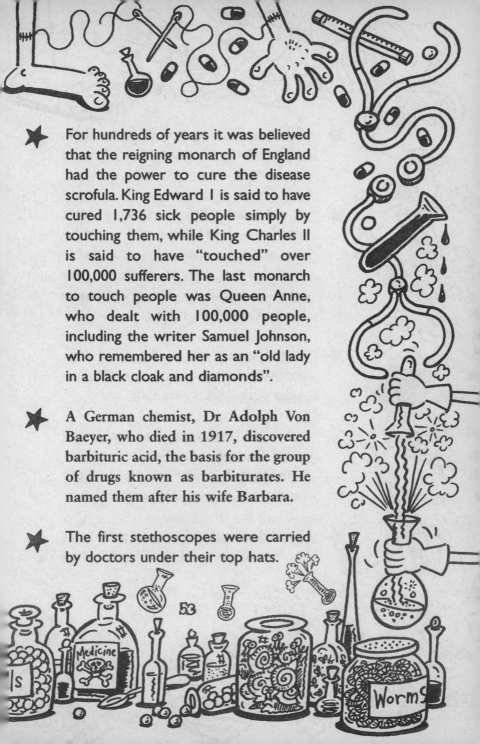

★ For hundreds of years it was believed that the reigning monarch of England had the power to cure the disease scrofula. King Edward I is said to have cured 1,736 sick people simply by touching them, while King Charles II is said to have "touched" over 100,000 sufferers. The last monarch to touch people was Queen Anne, who dealt with 100,000 people, including the writer Samuel Johnson, who remembered her as an "old lady in a black cloak and diamonds".

★ A German chemist, Dr Adolph Von Baeyer, who died in 1917, discovered barbituric acid, the basis for the group of drugs known as barbiturates. He named them after his wife Barbara.

★ The first stethoscopes were carried by doctors under their top hats.

★ When it first appeared, Coca Cola, without the fizz, was sold as a medicine.

★ In the past 500 years many great advances in medicine and everyday first aid could not have been possible without the use of scissors. They were invented by the great Italian genius Leonardo da Vinci.

★ The first patients to be fitted with artificial limbs by doctors lived in India over 3500 years ago.

★ Influenza is named after the Italian word for influence – based on the belief that flu epidemics were caused by the influence of particular stars.

★ The first dentists in Japan pulled out teeth with their fingers. They had to practise to make their fingers strong enough to do this.

★ The first spectacles to deal with poor eyesight were reported in Italy in 1289. It took until 1623 for lenses to be made to suit people who had varying degrees of problems with their eyes.

★ The first X-ray, by Wilhelm Roentgen, who had discovered these strange rays in 1895, was of his wife's left hand.

★ The "flying doctor" service was introduced to Australia in 1928.

★ The NHS (National Health Service) officially began in Britain on July 5 1948.

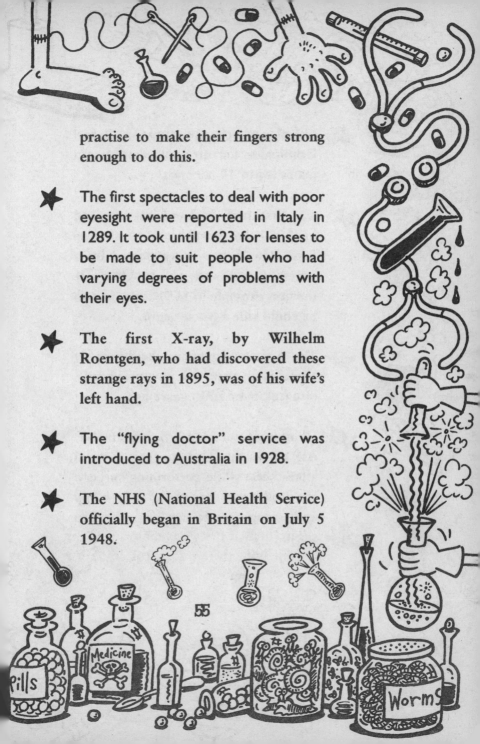

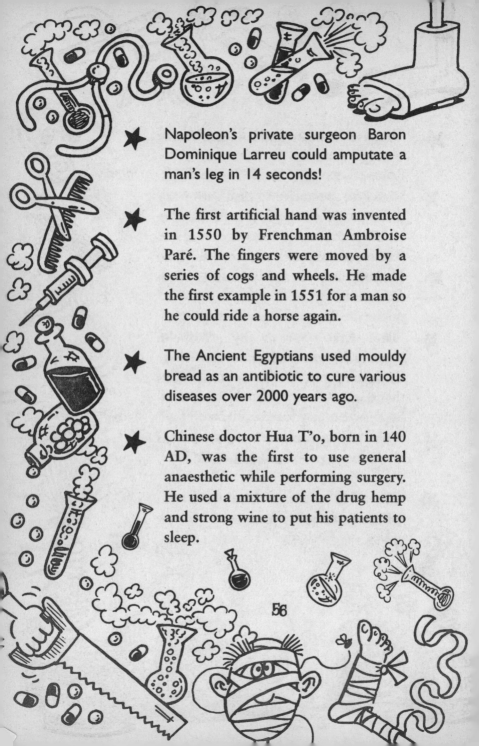

Napoleon's private surgeon Baron Dominique Larreu could amputate a man's leg in 14 seconds!

The first artificial hand was invented in 1550 by Frenchman Ambroise Paré. The fingers were moved by a series of cogs and wheels. He made the first example in 1551 for a man so he could ride a horse again.

The Ancient Egyptians used mouldy bread as an antibiotic to cure various diseases over 2000 years ago.

Chinese doctor Hua T'o, born in 140 AD, was the first to use general anaesthetic while performing surgery. He used a mixture of the drug hemp and strong wine to put his patients to sleep.

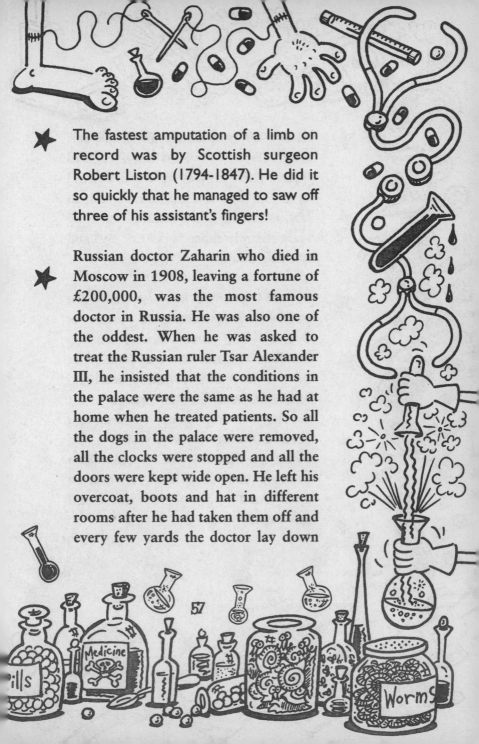

★ The fastest amputation of a limb on record was by Scottish surgeon Robert Liston (1794-1847). He did it so quickly that he managed to saw off three of his assistant's fingers!

★ Russian doctor Zaharin who died in Moscow in 1908, leaving a fortune of £200,000, was the most famous doctor in Russia. He was also one of the oddest. When he was asked to treat the Russian ruler Tsar Alexander III, he insisted that the conditions in the palace were the same as he had at home when he treated patients. So all the dogs in the palace were removed, all the clocks were stopped and all the doors were kept wide open. He left his overcoat, boots and hat in different rooms after he had taken them off and every few yards the doctor lay down

57

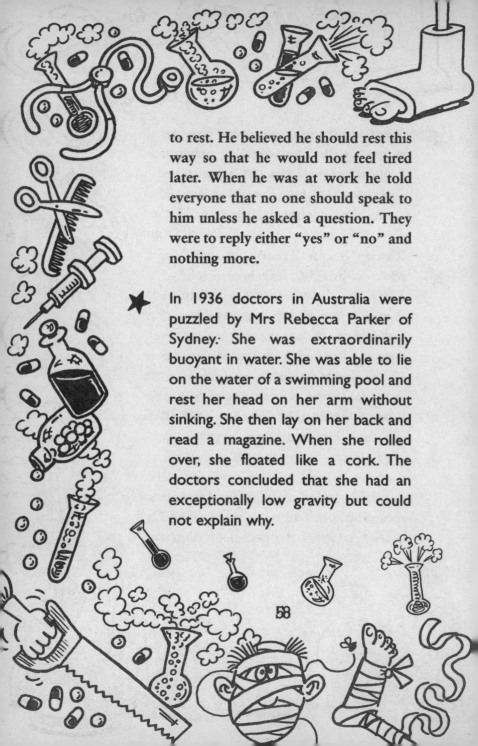

to rest. He believed he should rest this way so that he would not feel tired later. When he was at work he told everyone that no one should speak to him unless he asked a question. They were to reply either "yes" or "no" and nothing more.

★ In 1936 doctors in Australia were puzzled by Mrs Rebecca Parker of Sydney. She was extraordinarily buoyant in water. She was able to lie on the water of a swimming pool and rest her head on her arm without sinking. She then lay on her back and read a magazine. When she rolled over, she floated like a cork. The doctors concluded that she had an exceptionally low gravity but could not explain why.

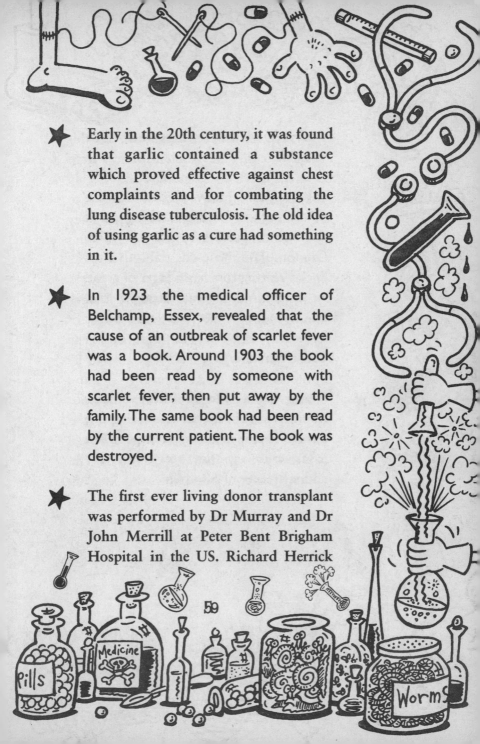

Early in the 20th century, it was found that garlic contained a substance which proved effective against chest complaints and for combating the lung disease tuberculosis. The old idea of using garlic as a cure had something in it.

In 1923 the medical officer of Belchamp, Essex, revealed that the cause of an outbreak of scarlet fever was a book. Around 1903 the book had been read by someone with scarlet fever, then put away by the family. The same book had been read by the current patient. The book was destroyed.

The first ever living donor transplant was performed by Dr Murray and Dr John Merrill at Peter Bent Brigham Hospital in the US. Richard Herrick was given a kidney by his twin brother Ronald.

★ For 15 years Meow-Meow was the official rat and mouse catching cat at the Whittington Hospital in north London. The hospital, named after Dick Whittington, has a logo of a cat. At one time it was thought that Meow-Meow's job was no longer necessary, but he was kept on by public demand.

★ During the last illness of King Charles II, his treatment for the remaining five days of his life included having red hot irons put on his feet and the administering of 58 drugs.

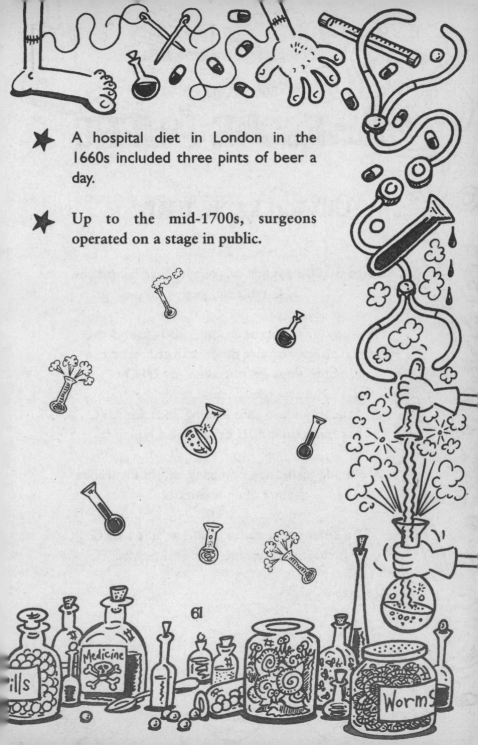

★ A hospital diet in London in the 1660s included three pints of beer a day.

★ Up to the mid-1700s, surgeons operated on a stage in public.

DID YOU KNOW THAT . . .

Up to 30,000 tonnes of cosmic dust fall on the
Earth each year.

A study by a doctor in the 1980s found that
small specks of dirt or dust in the eyes can
sometimes be mistaken for UFOs.

In Arès, France, a safe landing spot for UFOs
has been built. It is called the Ovniport.

A Florida insurance company offers insurance
against alien abduction.

The smells said to be inside an alien UFO
include sulphur, pepper and petrol.

Also published by Macmillan

FACT ATTACK

BEASTLY BODIES

DID YOU KNOW THAT . . .

The human body loses enough heat in an hour to boil half a gallon of water.

If calcium is taken out of human bones, they become so rubbery that they can be tied in a knot like rope or string.

The city with the highest number of babies born in taxis is New York, USA.

A giraffe has the same number of bones in its neck as a human does.

Richard III of England, Louis XIV of France and the Emperor Napoleon of France were all born with teeth.

Fact Attack titles available from Macmillan

The prices shown below are correct at the time of going to press. However, Macmillan Publishers reserve the right to show new retail prices on covers which may differ from those previously advertised.

Awesome Aliens	**Ian Locke**	**£1.99**
Beastly Bodies	**Ian Locke**	**£1.99**
Crazy Creatures	**Ian Locke**	**£1.99**
Fantastic Football	**Ian Locke**	**£1.99**
Dastardly Deeds	**Ian Locke**	**£1.99**
Cool Cars	**Ian Locke**	**£1.99**
Mad Medicine	**Ian Locke**	**£1.99**
Gruesome Ghosts	**Ian Locke**	**£1.99**
Dreadful Disasters	**Ian Locke**	**£1.99**
Nutty Numbers	**Rowland Morgan**	**£1.99**

All Macmillan titles can be ordered at your local bookshop or are available by post from:

Book Service by Post
PO Box 29, Douglas, Isle of Man IM99 1BQ

Credit cards accepted. For details:
Telephone: 01624 675137
Fax: 01624 670923
E-mail: bookshop@enterprise.net

Free postage and packing in the UK.
Overseas customers: add £1 per book (paperback)
and £3 per book (hardback).